How to Write a Great Book Report

A Workbooklet in Learning

By

Satiety McCollum

Copyright skbmccollum 2020

Table of Contents

Page 5 ..... There's an Easier Way

Page 9 ..... Now for the Filling

Page 15.... The Rest is up to You

Page 19 .. The End

There's an Easier Way

Do you have a book report coming up and you're a little nervous? Here is your relief. It's hard for those who think they can't write, but everyone has a good writer in them, if they look deep enough.

Sometimes people are stressed out about the word count, or the deadline, or of not being able to do a good job. With these simple directions you won't fear book reports any more, you'll be able to get right through them.

A lot of people think they should write their report after they've read the entire book, but you don't have to. There's an easier way that makes reading it more fun and you get to the end faster.

Write down the author's name, the year it was published and who published it, and how many pages the book has. This information needs to be just above the report itself.

Look at your book's table of contents and note the number of chapters and the names of them. You can use the chapter names in your report as sub-headings, which usually brings more points, or better grades.

Now, read the first chapter of the book and make notes about what happened in it. If you do this for each chapter your report will practically write itself, and you don't have to use everything you wrote down, but just as much as fits in the story. Don't forget character's names and a short description.

Now for the Filling

After this brief overview, we will look at a book report, so what isn't clear here, may clear up later.

Inside of the report you need to fill in all the details of the story using the notes you took after each chapter. Use descriptive, moving words, words that strike emotions. You want to SHOW the story rather than just TELL about it. If you can write something that makes the teacher want to read it, then you know you've done well.

Here's an example of telling:

She was so shocked by what she saw that instinct kicked in and she ran into the woods, where it was darker than dark.

Here's an example of showing:

She was so shocked that a rush of adrenaline coursed through her veins, and without thinking about it, she bolted. She ran as fast as she could without looking back until she reached the woods, where it got suddenly darker and colder.

Do you see the difference? Can you see her running scared in your head? Good writing will put your reader right in the story allowing them to 'see' it all.

Use the next pages to practice writing your rough draft.

The Rest is up to You

At the end, add a small paragraph saying what you thought of the book personally, and why you did or didn't like it. Did you love or hate the characters? Do you agree with the point of the book? Was it believable (if it was fiction)? Was it too short, too long? Say all the things you thought about. Be aware that this will add to your total word count.

Here's a sample report with notes.

"Adventures at the Ghost House"

By Satiety McCollum

Published by Independent Press 2020

134 pages

They Get to Clean

Mina and Corey get tricked by their drunken uncle Jack and now they have to clean the ghost house. Nobody's happy about it.

Alone in the Ghost House

Mina worked the first two days alone and was scared hearing noises all over the house. Doors slammed upstairs but there were no doors up there. Water faucets turned on by themselves, and horrific booms that rattled the windows, but couldn't be heard outside.

Finally, Help Arrived

On the third day of clean up, Corey decided to show up, and so did the landlord, who was a grumpy guy who's hair was always stringy and his dirty clothes didn't fit him. He yelled at them and the ghost stood up for them by throwing an old set of blinds on his head. The more he struggled, the more entangled he got. Mina and Corey laughed at him and he left angry.

Life Falls Apart for Mina

Mina ran away from home and thought she could live in the ghost house, as a last resort. Her only resort, really. Her mother was a hooker with a trail of men waiting, so she didn't spend any time or caring on Mina. Her first night in the ghost house she was nervous. She kept hearing a sound like a tiny kitten, so she got up to investigate and found a kitten she named G-Unit. It kept her company.

There's Good News and Bad News

Mina and Corey finished the house, and the property manager let Mina rent it. She went with him to sign papers, and when she got back, there were fire engines trying to put the house out. Mina freaked out and Corey had to hold her back from running into the house to save the kitten.

She didn't find the kitten, but her mother made compromises with her and convinced her to come back home.

<u>Greed and Jealousy</u>

A boy named Jack, who knew Mina and Corey from school, began stopping by to see Mina and Corey was jealous. Because he never really liked Jack and he also had unrequited feelings for Mina, it was hard for him to be nice to Jack. Mina had no idea that Corey loved her because he hid it to preserve their friendship. Jack comes by Mina's again when Corey was already there, and they went outside and fought in the street.

Two weeks later Mina received a check from an insurance company for being a fire victim. Mina paid her mother's rent for a year, and her and Corey got on a plane and never returned to Alaska. It's thought and hoped that they married and lived happily ever after.

The end, 134 pages

See, everything I'd written in the notes was used for my report, chapter by chapter. Taking and using notes one chapter at a time practically writes the report for you. Reading the entire book and then writing your report is a set up for forgetting some things that may be important in the report.

Some teachers give word limits on their book report assignments. If there's no word limit, then write as much or as little as you see is needed. However, if there is a word limit, there's a couple of ways to count the words so you can make sure you aren't short or over the limit.

One way is to remember this: one page written in 12pt. font (the size most widely used) is approximately 300 words, on average. You can count the pages for your word count, and a half a page would be 150 words. So if your report is 2 ½ pages, that would be 750 words, or 300 X 2 pages + 150 for the half page =750.

Another good (and easier) way is to use your word processor to count it. Most programs for writing have this feature. For instance, in Microsoft Word, click on the REVIEW tab at the top, and to the far left of the toolbar you'll see the button for word count. Click that and it'll tell you how many words are in the whole document, but if you highlight a paragraph and then click the word count button, it'll tell you how many words are in the highlighted area.

There are also websites where you can paste in your document and it'll tell you how many words are written. Here's a few of those, in case your word program doesn't offer a word count.

Wordcounter.net – this one is best, it counts the words, checks grammar and spelling, and even checks for plagiarism.

Countofwords.com – pretty basic word counter.

Nordictrans.com – offers what the others do but also offers a translation service, but it isn't free. Word counting is free, but if you want your document in French, you'll pay a minimal cost per word.

Wordcount.com – exactly what it says.

Use the grammar and spell checkers! I cannot stress that enough. You don't want to turn in a well-done report that's got misspellings and usage errors in it.

Besides, it makes the writer seem more educated when it's all done right.

You also don't want to seem too wordy. The most well-written works are written with only the necessary words to convey the message or story. For instance, scan over your document and look for phrases you can replace with a single word. Also take out any words that have nothing to do with the topic of the book. Example:

"Two weeks after the fire" can effectively be replaced with the word "later" or "after the fire". Look through your document for these nearly invisible mistakes and fix them, but make sure they sound natural in the sentence.

The End

It's okay – and many times preferred – that the writer give their opinion of the story at the end of the book report. It helps the reader to know that you read it to the end and that you really thought about what you read. If you choose to do this, make sure you aren't too wordy and try to keep your opinion to 100 words or less.

Here's an example of the last paragraph of your report:

I liked the story line but hated that nobody helped Mina. I strongly disagree with drinking alcohol, so the characters and I could never have been friends.

Or…

I think parents should call the police when their kids disappear, but nobody did when Mina ran away. She's a brave girl character who has her world by the horns, so to speak.

So you see, just a little bit about what you thought of the book as a reader is all that's necessary. Try to make an ending paragraph to this story as if you'd just read it by using the information provided here already. Use the next pages to practice on.

Other books by Satiety McCollum – all of which can be found at www.amazon.com/db/satietymccollum

Conversations with Two Eight Seven, 79 pages

This book is the true story of a family in Alaska that had to live with ghosts in a house they rented. Alaska is one of the most haunted places in the USA, except for the east coast, considering there was the peoples that first crossed the land bridge, then there was the gold rush, then the yellow peril, and then WWII when it was where they kept anyone they thought might have Japanese in them.

Then we also have the Native Peoples that settled and lived in Alaska. There was a lot of death in different periods of Alaska's history. You literally are never alone, and up North we found spirits in the wilderness, where nobody seemed to be.

This family moved into the town's most haunted house and had to learn how to live in Peace with them. The ghost with the most control taught them all kinds of things and insisted they call her a number, Two Eight Seven. This is the story of that family's adventure and discovery of the afterlife.

It's a short (79 pages) read that could be done in an evening, IF you're brave enough to read it before turning the lights out.

Gift-worthy Goods; Quality Gifts for a Couple of Bucks 125pgs

This book has projects for artwork that's nice enough to give away or sell. It contains easy instructions made with free or cheap items. People can use their SNAP benefits to get some of the supplies.

Your Inner Artist: Bring it Out 225pgs.

This book is intended to bring the artist out of the crafter. There are 15 projects and step-by-step instructions that are easy to follow, and the supplies come mostly from your home.

These are quality art pieces, and they don't look hand made if they're done well. The results are fine art that will impress you and your guests.

Study Aids: Workbooklets in Learning

This is an on-going project to help adults and middle schoolers in subjects that many students fine difficult. There are three in the series now, but more are coming very soon. Right now, available is:

How to Write a Great Book Report

How to Write a Poem

How to Write a Good Essay

<u>*NOTES*</u>

<u>*NOTES*</u>

<u>**NOTES**</u>

www.ingramcontent.com/pod-product-compliance
Lightning Source LLC
Chambersburg PA
CBHW071302130726
47998CB00003B/1300